G000141262

INSIDE A HOSPITAL

GILLIAN MERCER
ILLUSTRATED BY PETER DENNIS

Kingfisher Books

Educational advisers: Mary Jane Drummond,
Tutor in Primary Education,
Cambridge Institute of Education, Cambridge
Iris Walkinshaw, Headteacher, Rushmore Infants
School, Hackney, London

Technical advisers: Hazel Foale (Ward Sister)
Guy's Hospital, London; Pauline Shelley and
Jan Date, National Association for the Welfare
of Children in Hospital (NAWCH); Gay Oliver
(Physiotherapist) Moreton-in-Marsh Hospital

The author, illustrator and editor would also
like to thank Patty Preston and the
nurses and other staff at King's Mill Hospital,
Sutton-in-Ashfield, for their generous help in
the preparation of this book.

Kingfisher Books, Grisewood & Dempsey Ltd,
Elsley House, 24–30 Great Titchfield Street,
London W1P 7AD

First published in 1988 by Kingfisher Books

BRITISH CATALOGUING IN PUBLICATION DATA
Mercer, Gillian
Inside a hospital—(Stepping stones 4, 5, 6).
1. Hospitals—for children
I. Title II. Dennis, Peter III. Series
362 1'1
ISBN: 0 86272 360 4

Edited by Vanessa Clarke
Editorial Assistant: Camilla Hallinan
Cover designed by Pinpoint Design Company
Handwriting by Jack Potter
Phototypeset by Southern Positives and Negatives (SPAN),
Lingfield, Surrey
Colour separations by Newsele Litho Ltd, Milan
Printed in Spain

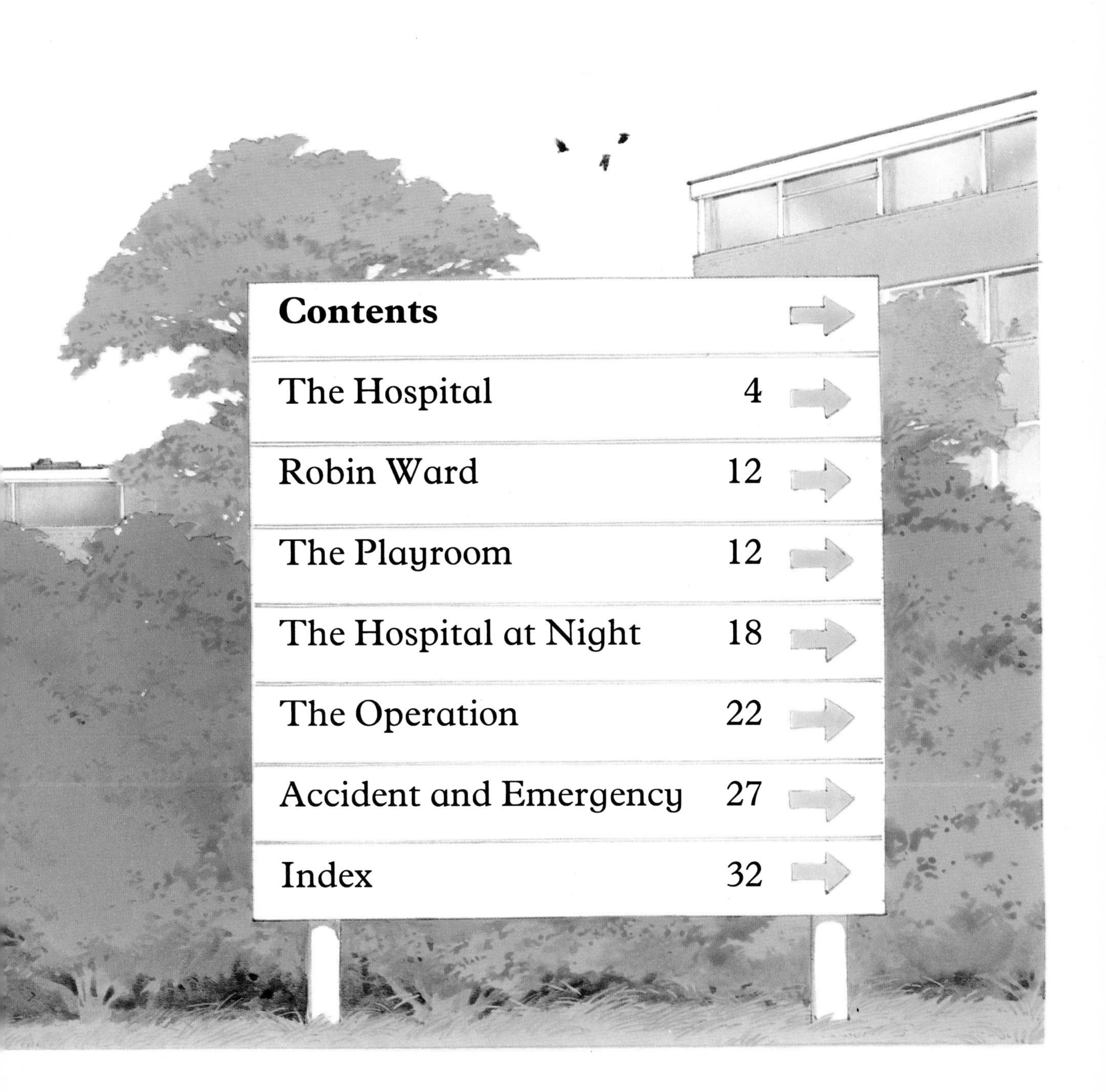

Contents

Here is the hospital. The people going through the doors have come because they are ill and the nurses and doctors will help them to get better. They are called patients while they are in hospital. Sometimes their families come with them too.

The first person the patients meet is Fred, the head porter, at Reception. He helps them to find the department they want. The hospital is like a large shop with many different departments. There are Operating Theatres where people have operations, X-ray Rooms where pictures are taken of people's insides, Maternity Units where babies are born, and rooms called Wards where patients rest in bed and sleep.

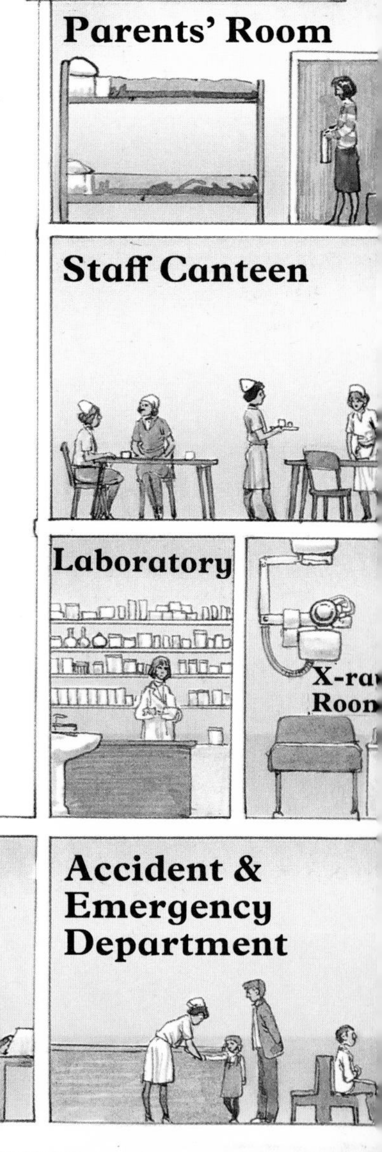

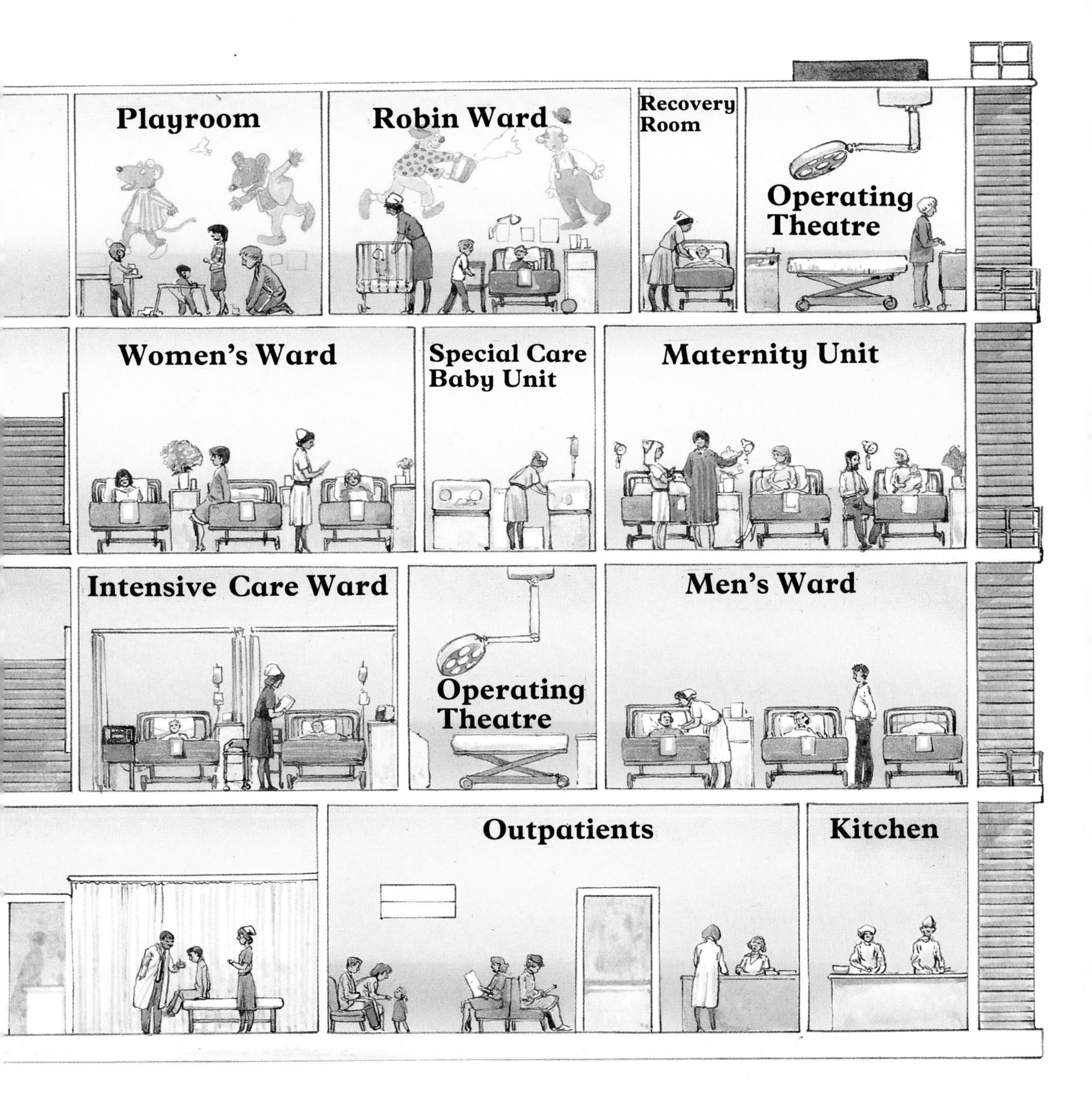
Playroom
Robin Ward
Recovery Room
Operating Theatre
Women's Ward
Special Care Baby Unit
Maternity Unit
Intensive Care Ward
Operating Theatre
Men's Ward
Outpatients
Kitchen

This is Robin Ward for children. Sister Carole is saying hello to Amy who has just arrived. Amy has come to hospital because she has a hernia which makes her tummy hurt. She will be having an operation to put it right. Sister Carole is in charge of the Ward. Martin has to stay in bed because his leg is broken, but everyone else is up.

F

Other nurses work in the Ward too. Helen is a staff nurse. She takes Amy's temperature with a thermometer to measure how hot her body is. She holds Amy's wrist and counts her pulse. The pulse is the throbbing beat you can feel on the inside of your wrist.

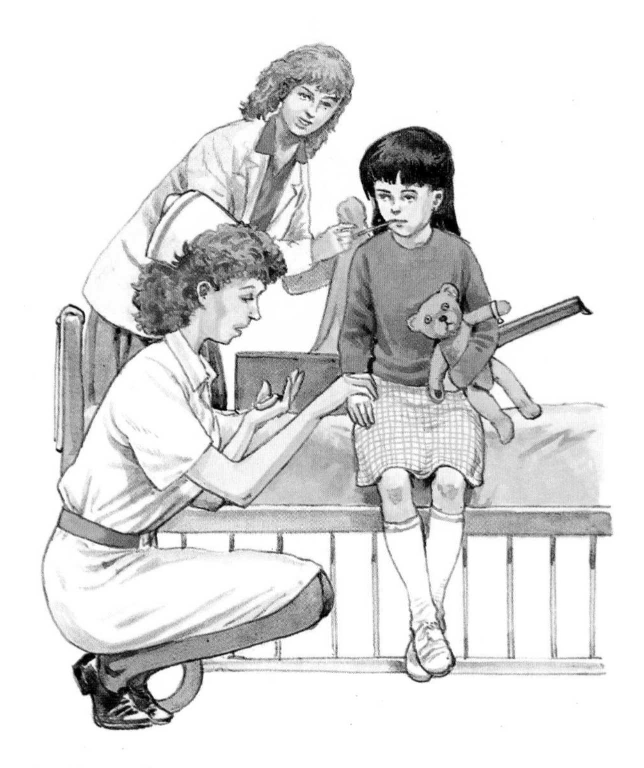

Amy's Mum unpacks Amy's clothes and toys. She is staying with Amy in the hospital.

Marie is still learning how to take care of patients. She is a student nurse. She writes Amy's name on a tag and fixes it around Amy's wrist. Amy's teddy gets a name tag too.

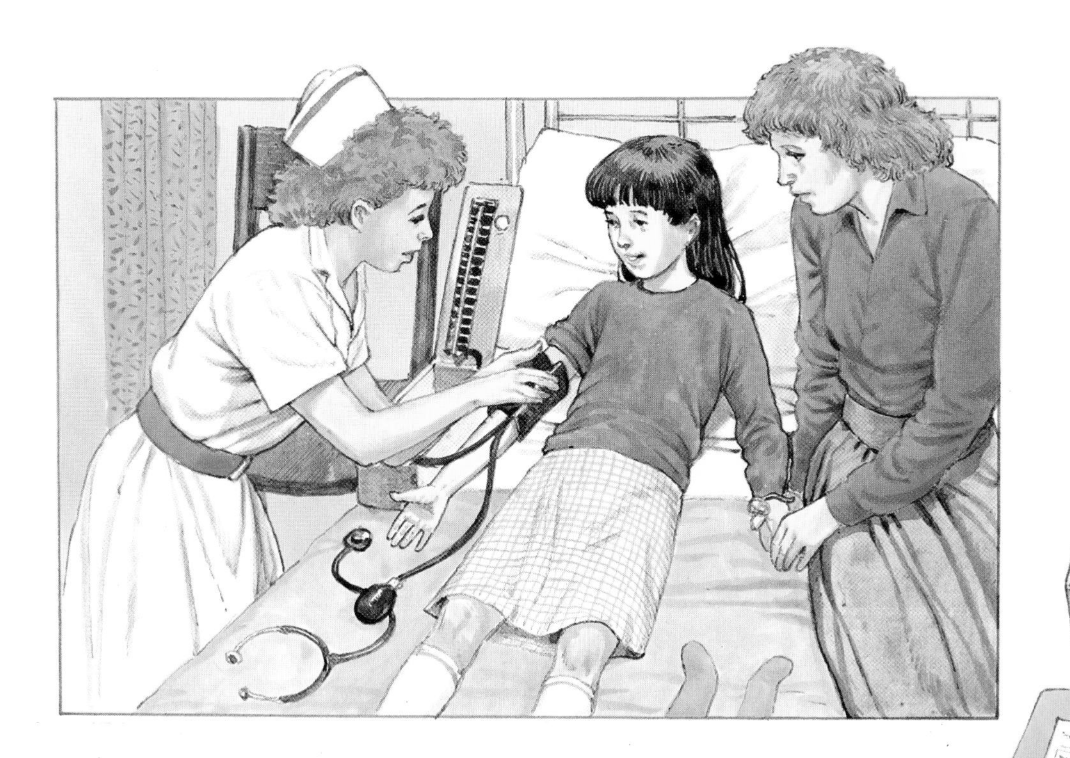

Nurse Helen takes Amy's blood pressure too. She wraps a cuff around Amy's arm and pumps air into it. An instrument connected to the cuff shows how fast Amy's blood is moving.

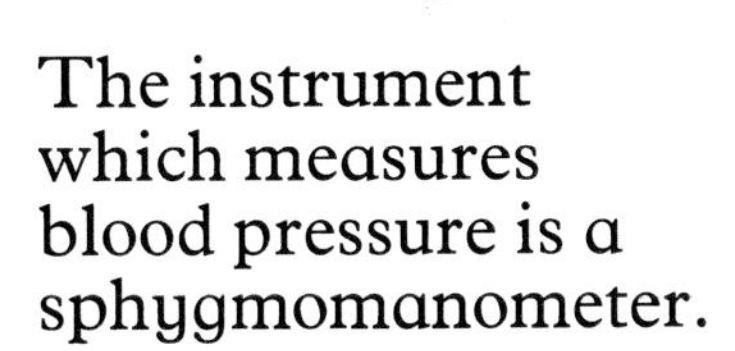

The instrument which measures blood pressure is a sphygmomanometer.

Helen writes down all the measurements on Amy's chart. The nurses take the measurements of all the children in the Ward at intervals during the day and check the charts to make sure they are getting better.

Here are the people who work with the nurses on the Ward.

Doctor Brown is the consultant. She listens to what Sister says and then decides the best treatment for each child.

Doctor Jim is a junior doctor. He comes to the Ward every day to check how well the treatment is working. He listens to the heart and lungs of the children with a stethoscope.

Victoria is the cleaner on the Ward. She makes the Ward bright and cheerful.

Sue's job is to play with the patients in the Ward. She brings books, paints and games to the Ward every day.

The children are playing with Sue in the Ward Playroom. She explains all about hospital treatment and gives them some real hospital equipment to use.

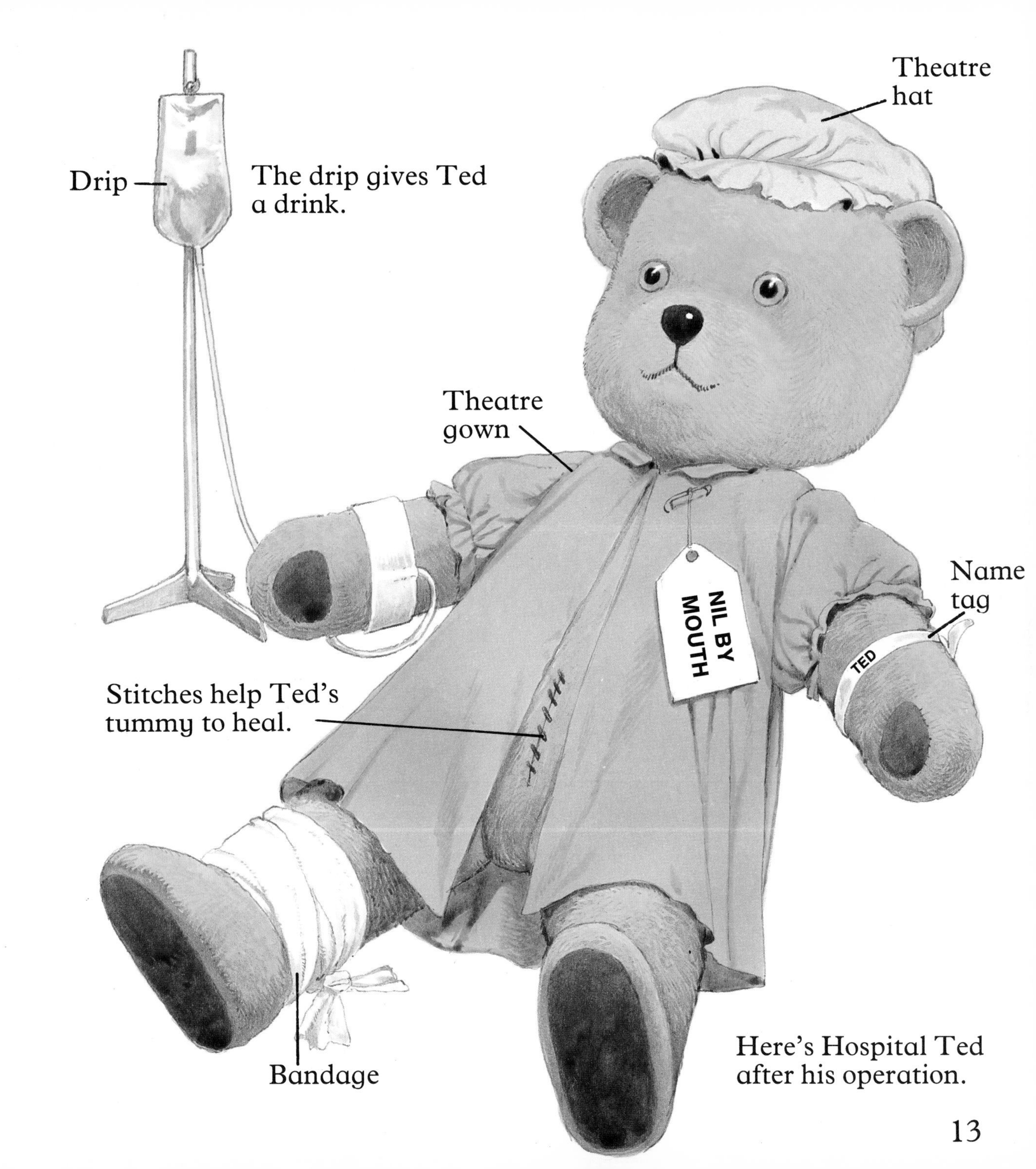
Theatre
hat
Drip
The drip gives Ted
a drink.
Theatre
gown
NIL BY
MOUTH
Name
tag
TED
Stitches help Ted's
tummy to heal.
Bandage
Here's Hospital Ted
after his operation.

The children eat their meals in the Playroom, unless they have to stay in bed like Martin. The nurses give them their lunch – parents can help too.

The kitchens in the hospital are enormous. A team of cooks makes all the meals for the patients. The children choose what they want from a menu.

David is the hospital teacher. He brings books and projects for children who have to stay in hospital a long time. Amy will only be in the hospital for two nights so she does not have to work with David unless she wants to.

Doctor Jim comes to tell Amy what will happen during her operation. A doctor called an anaesthetist will make her sleep. Then a doctor called a surgeon will operate on her tummy to repair the hernia.

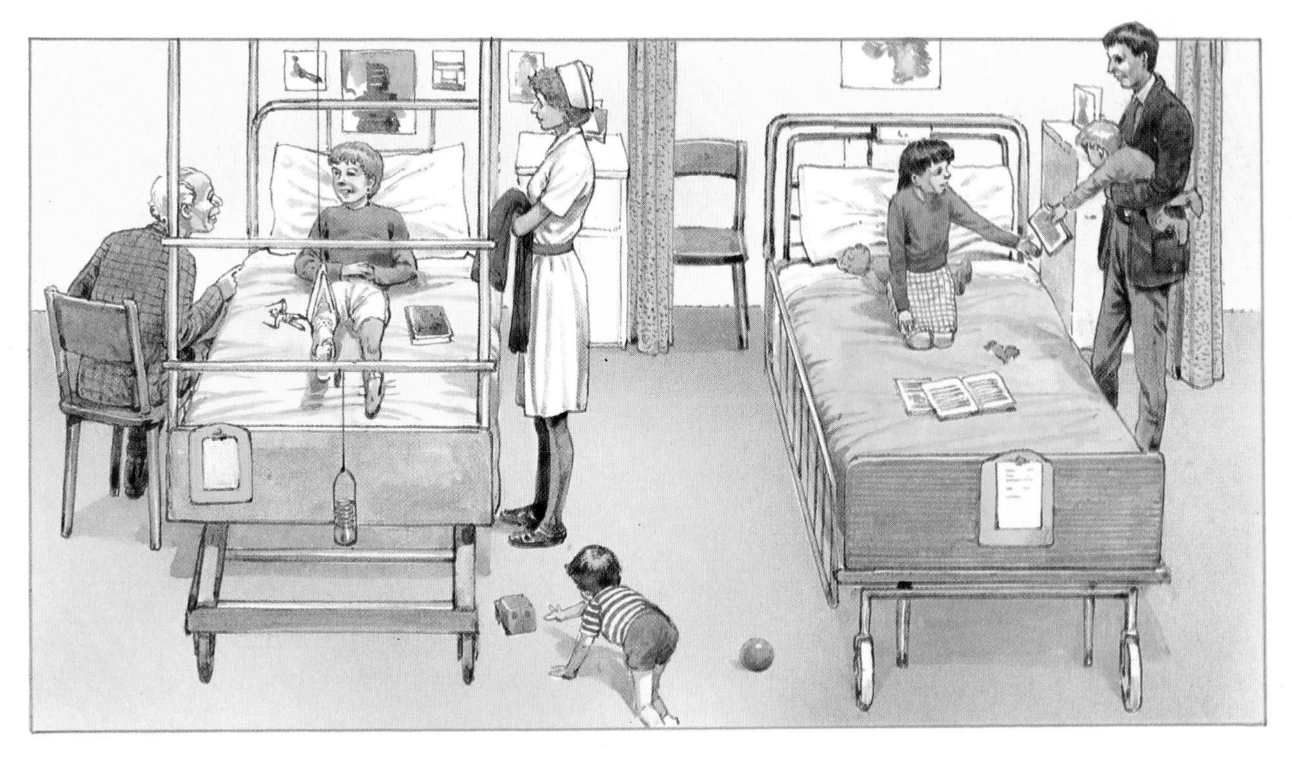

Some presents that visitors bring.

Amy's Mum can come into the Ward at any time but in the evening Amy's little sister and her Dad come to visit.

Then it is Amy's bedtime. Amy thinks her bed feels strange but her Mum sits beside her and she soon goes to sleep. Her Mum will sleep nearby. A night nurse stays in the Ward all night to make sure the children are sleeping peacefully. The nurses work in shifts so that there are nurses on duty all the time.

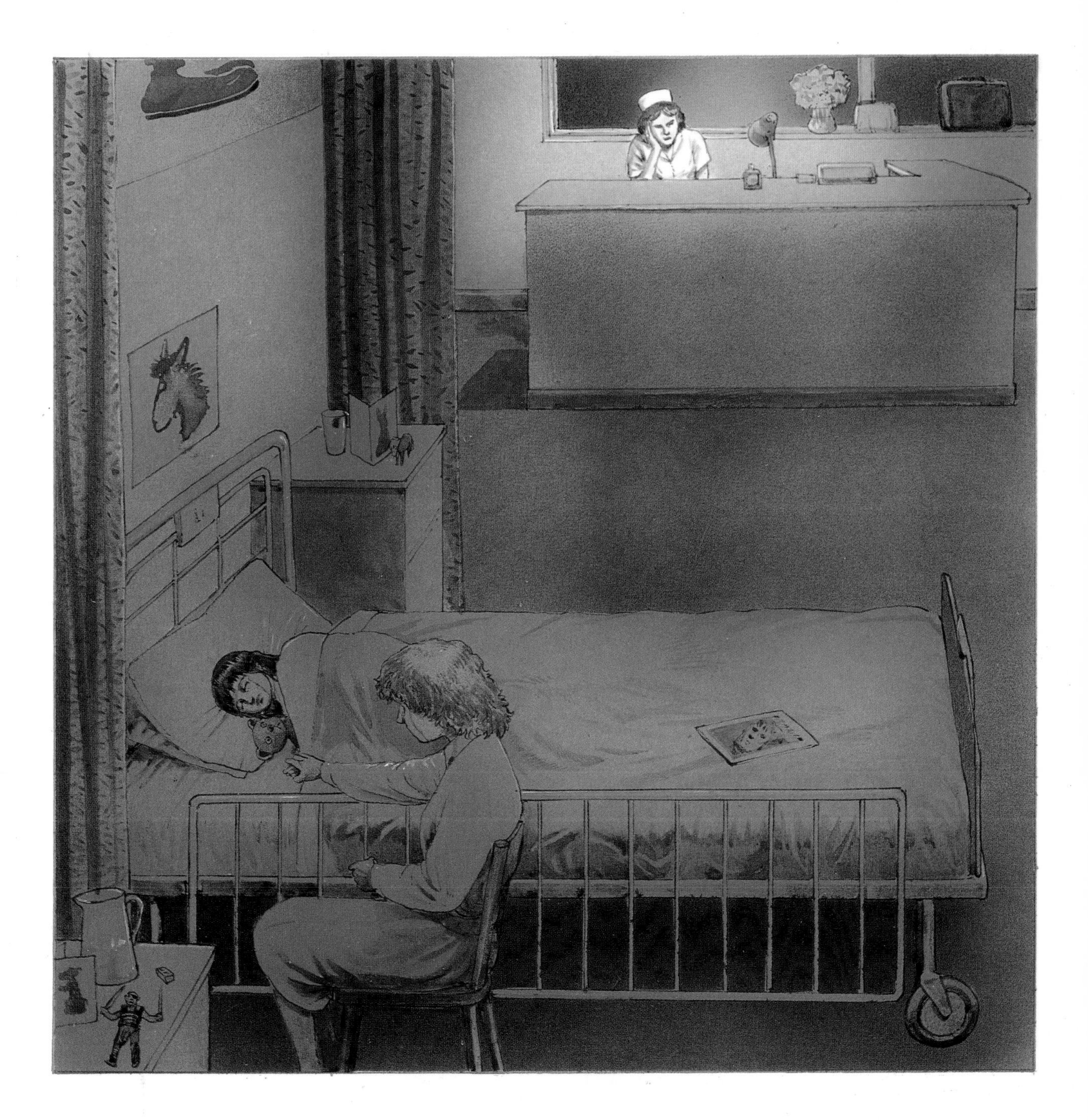

Not everyone in the hospital sleeps at night. In the Maternity Unit tiny babies wake to be fed. In the Intensive Care Ward doctors and nurses work hard all night looking after seriously ill patients. A telephone operator has to keep the telephones working in case there are any emergencies.

The Accident and Emergency Department is often busy. People can have accidents or become ill at any time of the day or night and must be rushed to hospital. If there is a real emergency an ambulance goes off at top speed to fetch the patient. The driver speaks to the hospital by radio so a nurse is waiting to help when they arrive with the new patient.

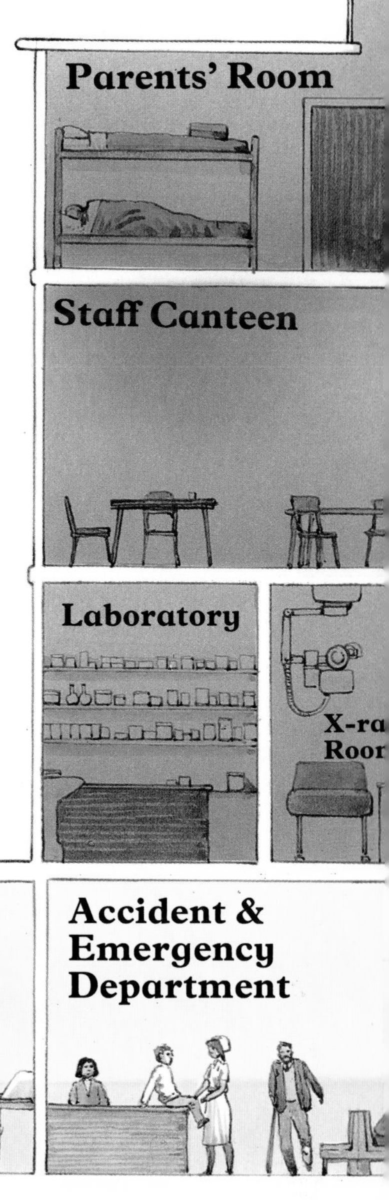

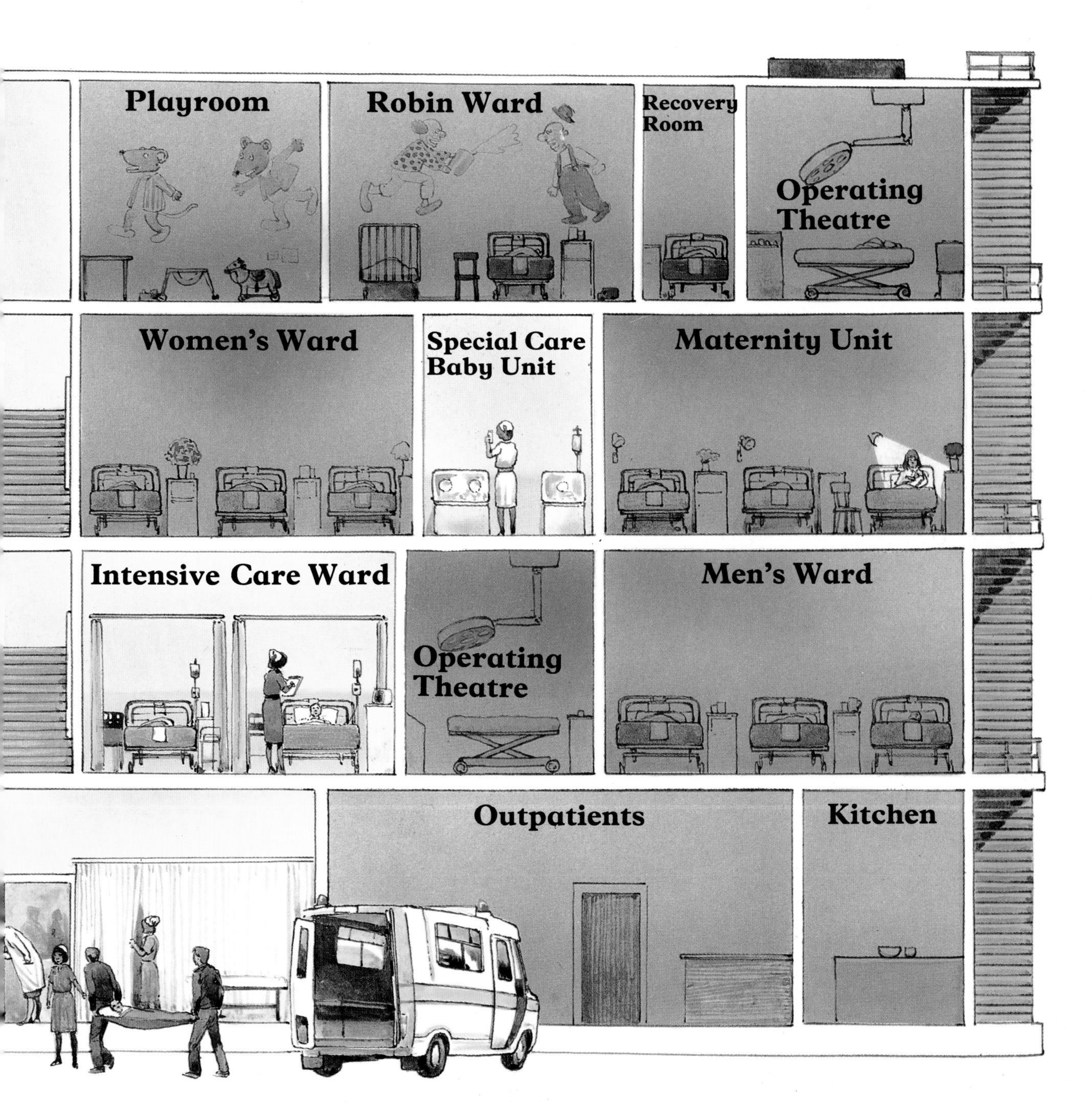
Playroom
Robin Ward
Recovery Room
Operating Theatre
Women's Ward
Special Care Baby Unit
Maternity Unit
Intensive Care Ward
Operating Theatre
Men's Ward
Outpatients
Kitchen
Ambulance

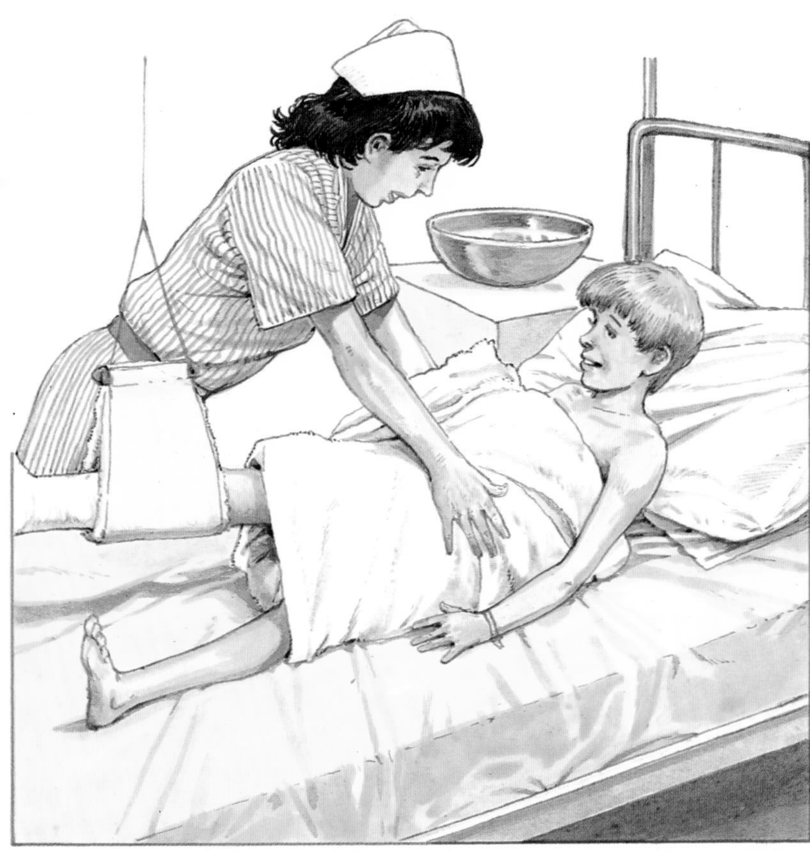

In the morning Amy isn't allowed any breakfast in case it makes her sick while she is in the Operating Theatre.

The nurses make the beds and make sure all the children wash. Martin can't go to the bathroom so Nurse Marie gives him a blanket bath. She covers him with towels and washes him bit by bit.

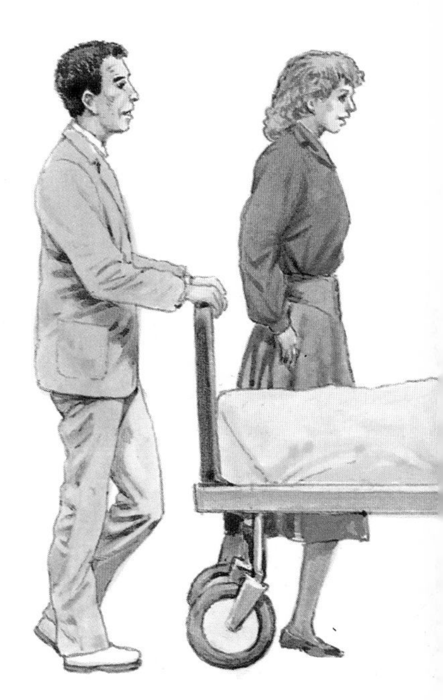

Now Amy is dressed in a theatre gown and hat, ready for her operation. Sister has given her a drink which will start to make her sleepy. Amy gives her teddy a drink too. She tells Sister that he is feeling sleepy.

A porter wheels Amy out of the Ward on her bed, and along to the Operating Theatre. Amy's Mum and Nurse Helen come with her.

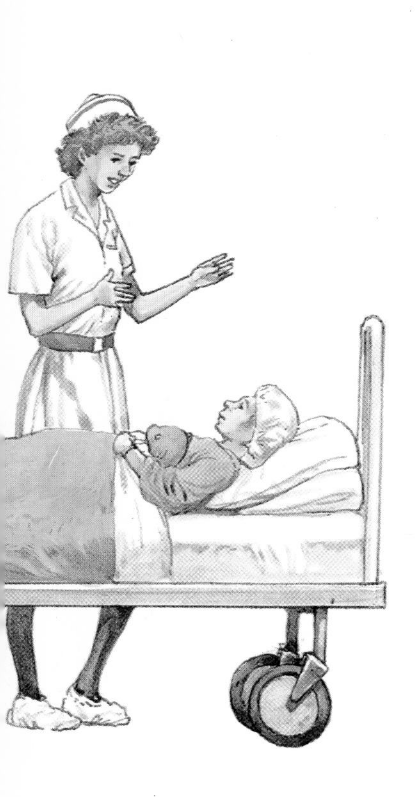

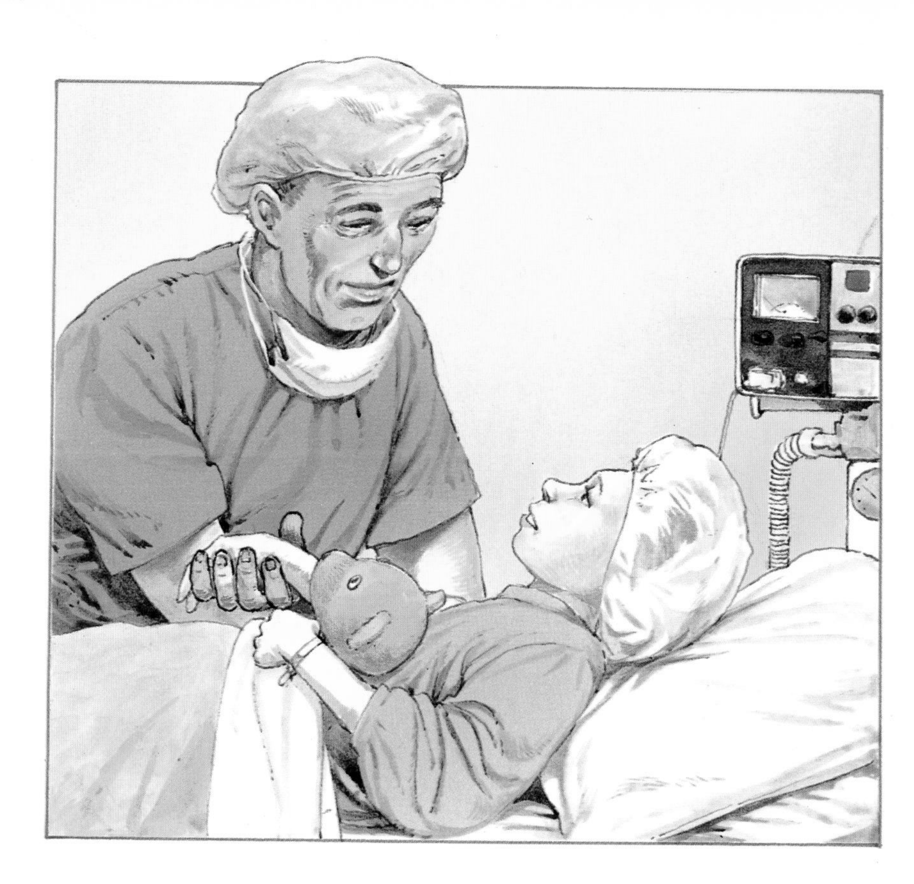

Nurse Helen goes with Amy into the Anaesthetics Room. By this time Amy is very sleepy. The anaesthetist explains that he will send her into a special kind of sleep. It is called anaesthesia. This means that the patient doesn't feel anything during the operation. The anaesthetist will stay with her all through the operation, checking her pulse and her breathing. After the operation she will wake up.

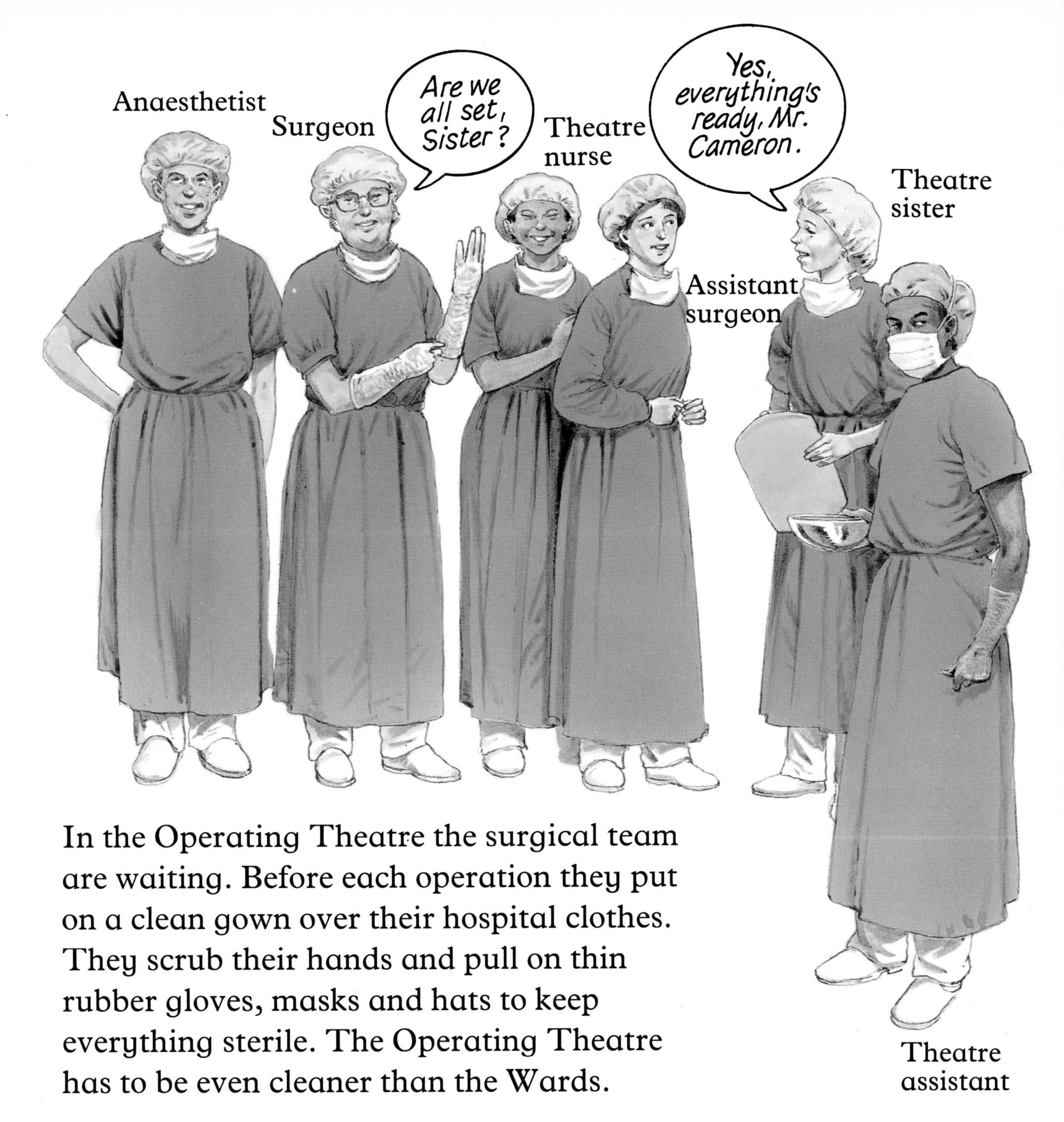

In the Operating Theatre the surgical team are waiting. Before each operation they put on a clean gown over their hospital clothes. They scrub their hands and pull on thin rubber gloves, masks and hats to keep everything sterile. The Operating Theatre has to be even cleaner than the Wards.

After the operation Amy is taken into the Recovery Room where she wakes up. She is still very sleepy because of the anaesthetic. Then a porter wheels her back to the Ward. The first person she sees when she wakes up again is her Mum.

The nurses are as busy as ever but Sister Carole stops to say hello. She and Nurse Marie are taking the medicine trolley around the Ward. Sister will look at the charts on the end of each bed to see what kind of medicine the doctors have written down for each patient. Some children can drink their medicine. Others swallow pills.

The physiotherapist is teaching Martin some exercises to keep his left leg strong while his broken leg mends.

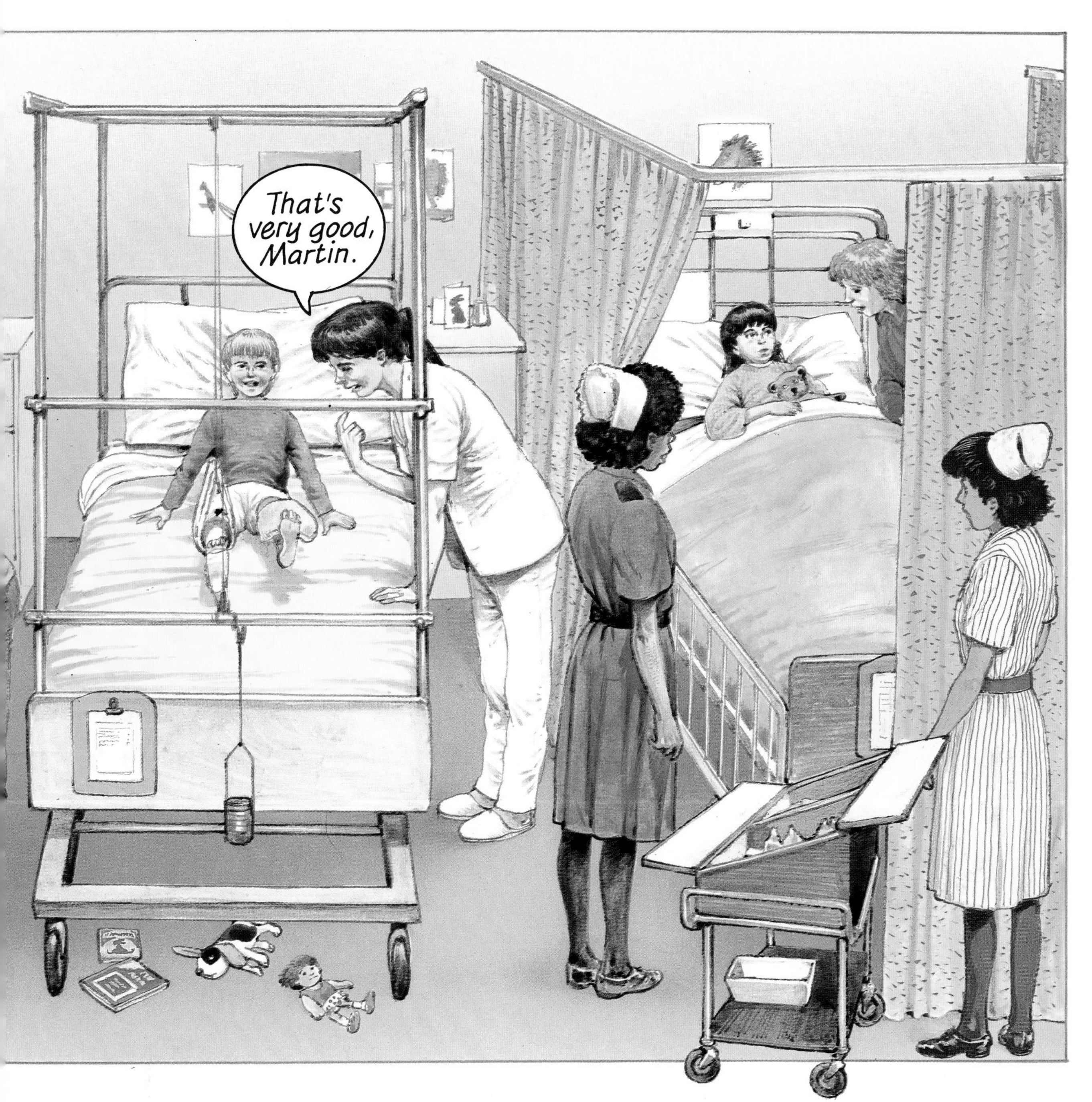
That's very good, Martin.

Next morning Amy asks for a big breakfast. She is very hungry even though her tummy is a little sore. Doctor Jim comes to see how she is feeling. He says that Amy is well enough to go home later today.

Amy has stayed two nights in hospital but many children come just to have treatment and then go home straightaway.

Joe fell off a climbing frame this morning. His hand is painful and a little bit swollen. So his mother has brought him to the Accident and Emergency Department. First they speak to the receptionist.

Then Doctor Paul examines Joe's hand. He decides that Joe should have an X-ray to make sure no bones have been broken.

In the X-ray Room the radiographer pulls down the big X-ray camera over Joe's hand. Then she stands behind a screen, and presses a button to take the picture. Her job is to use the X-ray machine to take different kinds of pictures of people's insides which will help doctors to understand what is wrong with their patients. Technicians develop the X-ray film just like a photograph taken by an ordinary camera.

Doctor Paul, Joe and his mother look at the X-ray picture. Good news – none of the bones is broken. Joe's hand is sore because he bruised it badly when he fell to the ground. It will soon get better.

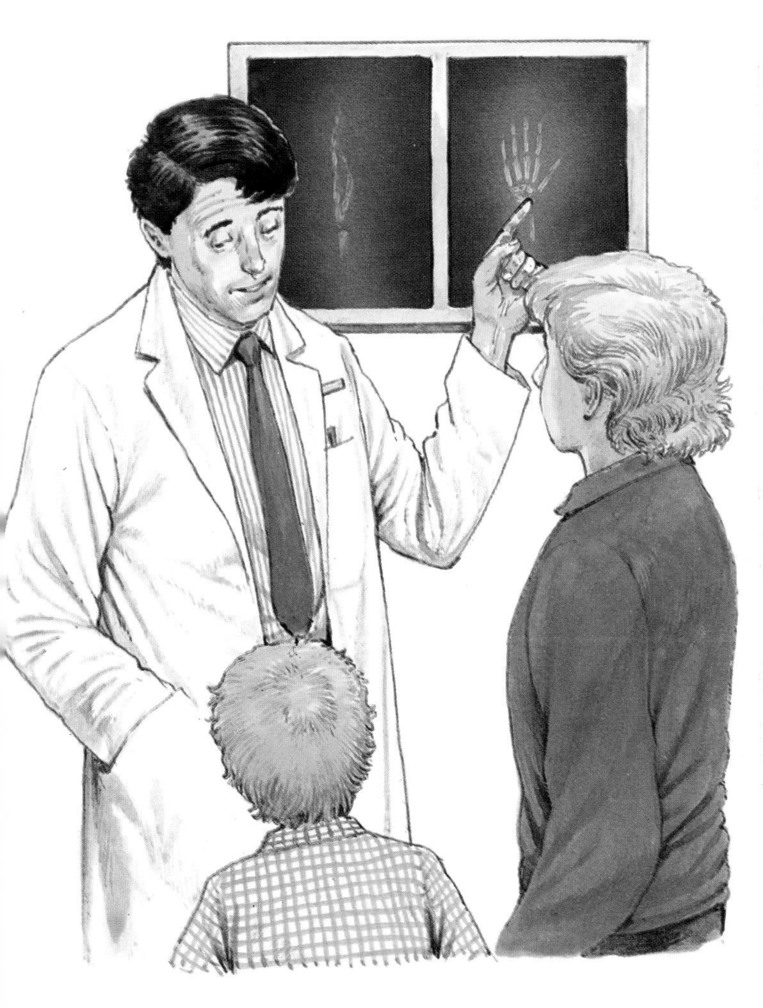

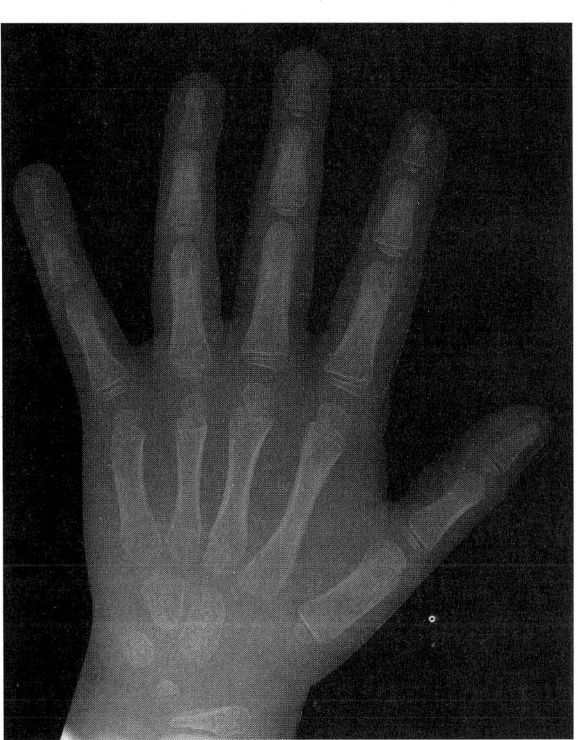

This X-ray shows all the bones inside a hand. None of them is broken.

Nurse Kevin puts a dressing on Joe's hand to keep it clean and winds a bandage on top to protect it.

Amy and Joe can both go home now but the hospital is still busy. More patients are arriving all the time. The nurses and doctors and all the other hospital workers will always be there, ready to take care of people when they are ill.

Accident &
Emergency
Reception
Robin Ward
Maternity Unit
X-ray Rooms

Index

NAWCH (The National Association for the Welfare of Children in Hospital) at Argyle House, 29–31 Euston Road, London NW1 2SD (tel 01-833 2041) is happy to offer information and advice to children going into hospital.

Numbers in Your Head

games and activities for children, using mental mathematics

John Spooner

ISBN 1 874099 73 1
Edited and typeset by Fran Mosley
Cover and illustrations by Andy Martin
Designed by Bookcraft, Stroud
Printed by Astral Printing, Stroud, using recycled paper

Contents

Brick Walls

for 1 person or 2 people working together

You need paper and pencil

Draw a simple wall like this.

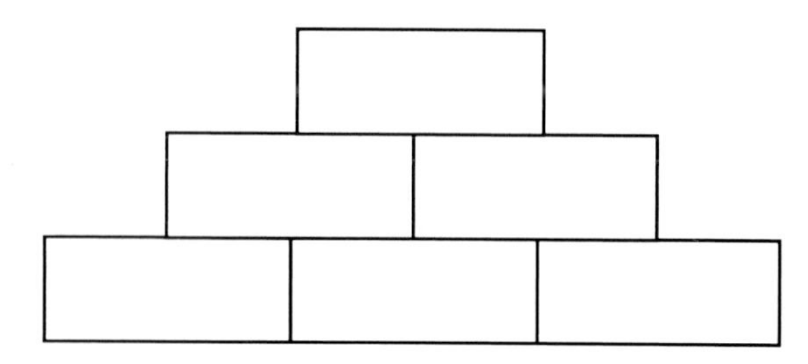

Choose three numbers and write them on the bricks at the base of the wall.

Add each pair of numbers and write the answers on the bricks above.

Then add *those* two numbers. Again, write the answer on the top brick.

Sally chose 3, 11 and 6.

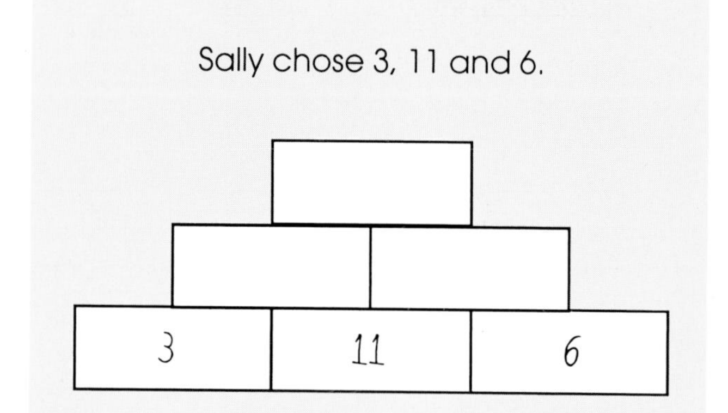

She added 3 and 11 to make 14.

Then she added 6 and 11 to make 17.

Then she added 14 and 17 to make 31.

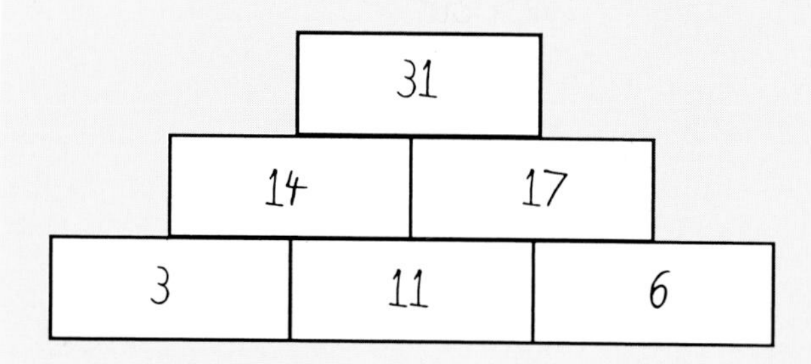

Questions

Where would you place the numbers at the base of the wall to make sure you get the highest number at the top?

What are all the different top-numbers you can get with your same three base-numbers?

Find all the possibilities.

What happens if you choose three consecutive numbers (say, 10, 11 and 12)?

Or three odd numbers?

Or three even numbers?

Variations

What numbers do you need at the base to make a top brick of 30?

What are all the possibilities?

Use higher numbers — or decimal numbers or fractions.

Make a wall with a four-brick base — or a five-brick base.

Subtraction Walls

for 1 person

You need paper and pencil

Draw a simple wall like this.

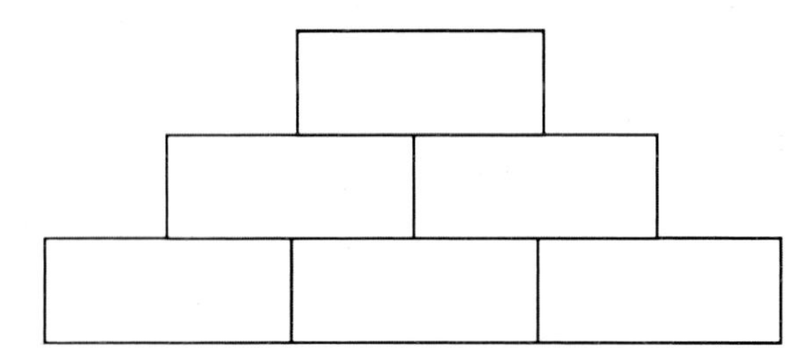

Choose three numbers and write them on the bricks at the base of the wall.

Find the difference between each pair of numbers and write the answers on the bricks above.

Then find the difference between *those* two numbers. Again, write the answer on the top brick.

Mettan chose 5, 9 and 11.

5	9	11

He subtracted 5 from 9 and got 4.

Then he subtracted 9 from 11 and got 2.

Then he subtracted 2 from 4 and got 2.

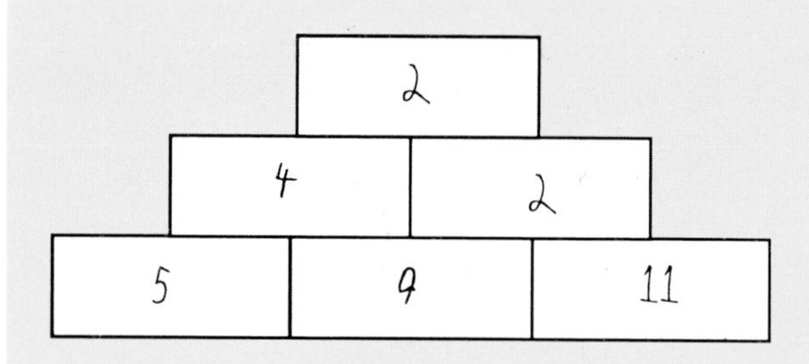

Questions

How many different numbers can you get on the top brick by using the same three numbers on the base?

What happens if you subtract the larger number from the smaller in each pair?

How can you end up with a total of 12 (or 100 or 500) on your top brick?

What numbers are at the base?

What happens if you choose three odd numbers?

Or three even numbers?

Variations

Rub out one or two numbers from your completed wall and get a friend to work out what numbers are missing.

Aim to get zero as the number on the top brick.

Try using multiples of the same number on the base bricks (for example, 4, 8 and 16).

What do you notice?

for 4 to 6 people

You need squared paper (biggish squares)
pens or pencils

Decide who is the caller. That person needs this book.

Everyone else needs a sheet of squared paper with just six squares.

Caller:

- slowly read out the numbers in the box on this page

Other players:

- choose six of the numbers the Caller says, and write them in your six squares; make sure you don't just pick the first six

Now you are all ready to play.

Caller:

- pick one of the numbers from the box and read it out slowly

Other players:

- if you have that number on your sheet, cross it off

Everyone carries on like this until somebody has all six numbers crossed off. They win.

397 279·6 999
400 6·4 1000·25
2641
1001 654 82·1
89·2
100·2 70·5
1221 1·05

Variations

Write the numbers up on the board for everyone to see; choose six of them to write in your squares.

Caller, instead of reading out a number you can say things like "The smallest number" or "1000 minus 1".

Use simple two-digit numbers.

Use a wider range of numbers.

Make 10

for 2 people

You need two sets of number cards 0 to 10
sand timer
an answers chart (optional)

Choose who will be the Dealer and who will be the Caller. The aim is to get all the answers right before the sand runs through.

Dealer:

➤ shuffle together all the number cards and put them in a pile

➤ pick the top card and put it face up on the table

➤ start the sand timer as soon as you have placed the first card on the table

Caller:

➤ call out the number which will give 10 when added to the number on the card

➤ now say the whole calculation: "... and ... make ten"

Dealer:

➤ you must only turn over the next card when the Caller has said the calculation correctly

If the first answer is wrong, the Caller must try again to find the correct answer.

Both of you, carry on like this until the cards are all used up. Does the Caller manage to do it in time?

Now swap over and play again.

The Dealer put down a 7, so Mettan said "Three; because 3 and 7 make ten".

Questions

How many different pairs of numbers can be added to make 10?

If you play this game several times, does your time improve?

Can you design a graph to keep track of your times?

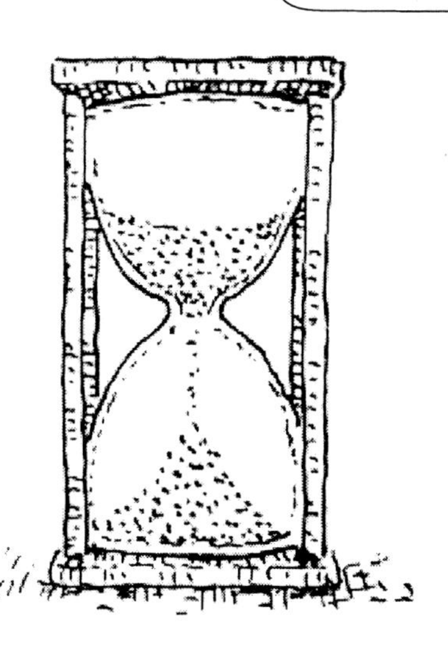

Variations

Play Make 20. In this game you must make the card-number and the number you call add up to 20.

Play Take 10, where you take the number on the card away from 10 and call out the answer.

Use cards numbered 0 to 5 and deal two cards at a time. The Caller has to add the two card-numbers on the table and call out the number needed to make 10.

Play Make 100, using number cards 0 to 50.

Make 10 Challenge

for 3 people

You need number cards 0 to 10
an answers chart (optional)

Choose who will be the Dealer.
The other two players are Callers.

Dealer:

➤ shuffle the cards and put them in a pile

➤ pick the top card and put it face up on the table between the two Callers

Callers:

➤ call out the number which will give 10 when added to the number on the card

Sally put down a 6, so the Caller said "Four" (because 6 + 4 = 10).

Dealer:

➤ give the card to whoever gives the correct answer first

➤ you must only turn over the next card when the correct number has been called (if necessary, the Callers must try another answer)

All of you, carry on like this until the cards are all used up.

At the end of the game add up the numbers on your cards.
The person with the highest total is the winner.

Swap the jobs around and play again.

Variations

Dealer, pick one card from a set showing 1, 2, 3, . . . ,9 and another card from a set showing 0·1, 0·2, 0·3, and so on.

Callers, add the two numbers and call out the third number which must be added to make 10.

Play Make 12, or Make 7 or . . .

Design a different (fairer?) scoring system.

Play Make 100, using number cards 0 to 50.

Quick as a Flash

for 2 people

You need two sets of number cards 0 to 10
stopwatch
answer chart or calculator (optional)

Decide who is the Dealer and who is the Caller.

Decide what type of number operation (+, × or –) you are going to use for the game.

Dealer:

- ➤ shuffle all the number cards together and put them in a pile
- ➤ pick the top two cards and put them face up on the table
- ➤ start the stopwatch immediately

Caller:

- ➤ look at the card-numbers
- ➤ do the operation in your head as quickly as you can, then say the calculation out loud

Dealer:

- ➤ you must only turn over the next cards when the Caller has given the correct answer

Both of you:

- ➤ carry on like this until you have used up all the cards
- ➤ stop the watch when the Caller has given the last answer

Now swap over and play again. Which of you is quicker?

8 6

Sally and Mettan decided to do subtraction.

The first two numbers were 8 and 6, so Sally said "Eight minus six is two".

Variations

Use number cards 0 to 20 or 0 to 30.

Use two piles of number cards and pick one from each pile.

One pile could have fractional or decimal numbers (such as ½ or 2·4), and the other could have whole numbers.

Try using division too.

Can you do the division calculations in your head, or do you need to use a pen and paper, or a calculator?

Questions

Which number operations are the easiest and which are the hardest?

Which operation allows more than one correct answer when you play this game?

Tables Chase

for 3 people

You need two sets of number cards 0 to 10
paper and pencil for keeping scores
calculator

Decide who is the Dealer. The other two players are the Callers.

Dealer:

- shuffle together all the number cards and put them in a pile
- turn over the top two cards and put them on the table

Callers:

- you must multiply the numbers on those two cards and call out the answer
- the first person who gives the correct answer scores that many points

Dealer:

- check that the answers are correct (you can use the calculator if you want to)
- when all of the cards have been played, shuffle them and start turning over two at a time again

The first player to reach 200 is the winner.

When you have finished, swap jobs and start again.

The cards 5 and 8 were played, so Mettan called 40 (because $5 \times 8 = 40$).

He said it before Sally, so he scored 40 points.

Questions

Does this game show you which tables you need to practise?

If so, which ones are they?

Do you think the zero card should be included in the game?

Why?

Might you ask those people who always win to share the secrets of their success with you?

Variations

Allow both of the Callers more time to work out the answer.

They could both write down the answer on paper and show it to the Dealer.

If they are both correct then they could both win points.

Use different sets of cards — perhaps 0 to 15 or 0 to 20.

Use two piles of cards and pick one card from each pile.

One pile could have decimal numbers such as 3·6 or 9·1.

Odds and Evens Race

for 2 people

You need two sets of number cards 0 to 10
paper and pencil for keeping scores

Decide who will collect odd numbers and who will collect even numbers.

Shuffle the number cards and deal them all out so you have ten each.

Both players:

- put your cards in a pile face down on the table
- turn over one card each and say the numbers

The Odd Person goes first.

Odd Person:

- if you can, do an operation with those two numbers that will produce an odd number (you can use + or × or – or ÷)
- whatever the answer is, that is how many points you score — as long as it is odd

Even Person:

- now you use the same two numbers, and try to do an operation that will give an even number
- whatever the the answer is, that is your score — as long as it is even

When all the cards have been used, shuffle them and give each player ten cards again.

The first player to reach 100 or over is the winner.

7 2

Sally was the Odd Person.

The cards 7 and 2 were turned over.

She chose to do 7 + 2 = 9 and scored 9 (because, of course, 9 is odd).

Questions

Is it easier for the Even Person or the Odd Person to win?

What happens when you multiply an even number by an even number?

And when you multiply an odd number by an odd number?

Is it ever impossible to make an even number?

Or an odd number?

Does zero count as odd or even?

Why do you think that?

Variations

Use cards with higher numbers, such as 10 to 20.

Play with three players, so that each time there are three cards on the table.

You can then do mixed operations, like this:

$(4 + 6) \times 3 = 30$

Some Sum

for 2 people

You need calculators
paper and pencil

Both players:

➤ write down five calculations like this

$$14 \times 11 = 154$$

$$12 \times 23 = 276$$

$$60 \div 3 = 20$$

or even like this

$$(14 \times 11) + 3 = 157$$

➤ then write them out again, on a fresh sheet of paper; this time miss out part of the calculation (either a number or the operation sign) and draw a box for your partner to fill in instead

➤ decide if you will let your partner use a calculator

➤ swap papers and write in the missing bits

Mettan worked out on his calculator that $14 \times 11 = 154$.

He could write this down as a calculation for Sally in one of these ways:

$$\square \times 11 = 154$$

$$14 \times \square = 154$$

$$14 \ \square \ 11 = 154$$

Questions

Can addition help to solve a subtraction calculation?

If so, how?

Can multiplication help to solve a division calculation?

If there is more than one number operation in the calculation, does the order in which the operations are carried out affect the answer?

Why?

Variations

Write down ten calculations — or even 15!

Explain to your partner how you worked out the missing bits.

Decide together on a number, and then race to write down ten calculations that give that number.

For example, if the number is 25 you could write

$50 \div 2$

$100 - 75$

and so on.

Use decimal numbers, or fractions.

Magic Squares

for 1 person

You need three sets of number cards 0 to10 (about 3 cm × 3 cm square)

Choose three consecutive numbers from your set of cards. ('Consecutive' means 'one after the other' — for example, you might choose 1, 2 and 3, or 7, 8 and 9.)

Pick out all the cards with those numbers on them — make sure you have three of each.

Place these cards anywhere on the grid.

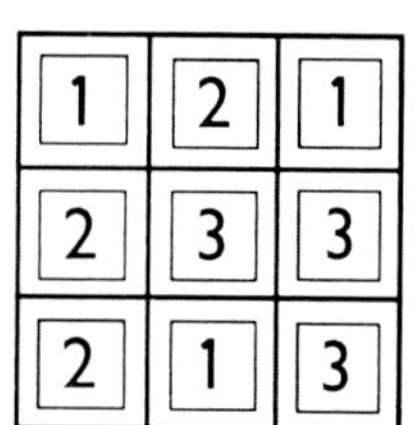

Now try to rearrange the cards to make a magic square — that is, so that *every* row, column, and diagonal adds up to the same total.

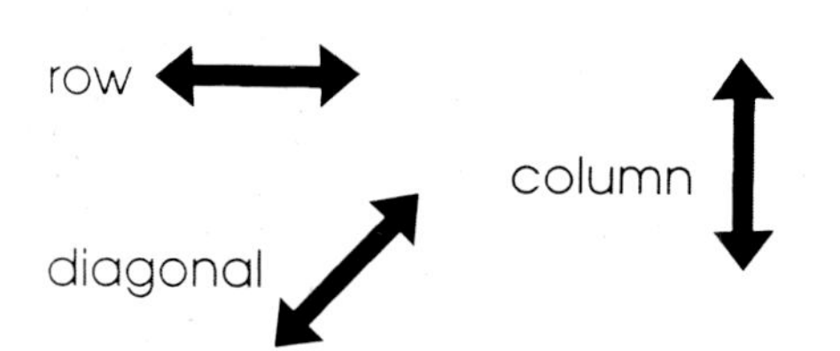

Questions

Can you arrange the cards in more than one way to make the square magic?

Where do the highest and lowest numbers need to go each time in order to make the square magic?

Does **any** set of nine numbers produce a magic square?

Can you find the rule which allows non-consecutive numbers to produce magic squares?

Can **any** set of three consecutive numbers make a magic square?

What about consecutive odd (or even) numbers?

Variations

Try using four consecutive numbers in a 4 × 4 grid, or five numbers in a 5 × 5 grid.

Try using non-consecutive numbers on a 3 × 3 grid.

2, 5 and 8 can be arranged into a magic square but 2, 5 and 7 cannot. Why is that?

Try using nine *different* numbers in a 3 × 3 grid.

Doubling

for 2 people

You need calculator
paper and pencil

Decide who is going to have the calculator. They are the Calculator Person.

Non-calculator Person:

➤ choose a number under 20 and write it down

➤ tell your partner what it is

Both players:

➤ double the number and write down the answer — the Calculator Person must use the calculator and make the answer show in the display; the Non-calculator Person must use their head

Calculator Person:

➤ when you have found the answer, don't say what it is until the Non-calculator Person has found their answer

Both players:

➤ keep doubling the number and writing the answer until the Non-calculator Person makes a mistake; then you stop

Swap jobs and play again.

SCORING

The Non-calculator Person scores whatever number was their last correct answer.

The Calculator Person scores nothing this time round (but they will next time).

Questions

Have you discovered any tricks or patterns that help you work out the answer quickly?

Can you write them down or explain them to a friend?

If you can double 2, 4, 6 and 8 easily, would it also be easy to double 20, 40, 60 and 80?

Does knowing how to double 1, 5 and 7 help you to double 157?

If so, how?

What about doubling 1570?

Once you start doubling, how many odd numbers do you make?

Why is that?

Variations

Instead of doubling, keep adding a certain number to your starting number.

Start with a decimal number (such as 2.5) or a negative number.

Instead of doubling you have to treble the numbers.

Start with one of these numbers and keep halving: 48, 192 or 1536.

Or try 10, 100 or 1000.

Double Digit

for 1 person or 2 people working together

You need paper and pencil
calculator (optional)

Choose two digits and arrange them to make two double-digit numbers.

> Sally chose 1 and 2 as her digits and arranged them to make 12 and 21.
>
> 1 and 2
>
> 12 and 21

Now add your double-digit numbers

> Sally added 12 and 21.
>
> $12 + 21 = 33$

Now add your single-digit numbers

> Sally added 1 and 2.
>
> $1 + 2 = 3$

Now divide your double-digit answer by your single-digit answer.

> Sally divided 33 by 3.
>
> $33 \div 3 = 11$

Try lots of examples and see what happens.

Can you explain what is happening?

Questions

What happens if you choose zero as one of your digits?

Can you do it with negative numbers?

What happens if you use two of the same single digits — for example, 5 and 5?

Variations

Try the same investigation using three digits. (You should be able to make six different three-digit numbers.)

Do you get the same results from the investigation?

Use four single-digit numbers and try the same investigation.

(You will have to be very organised.)

Do you get similar results?

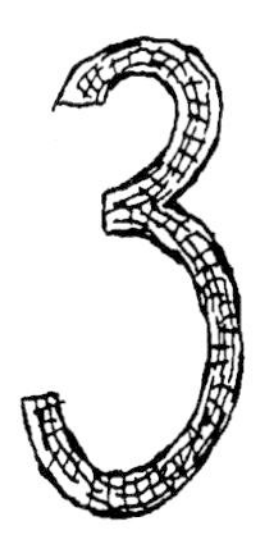

Sharing

for 1 person

You need calculator
record sheet divided into three columns

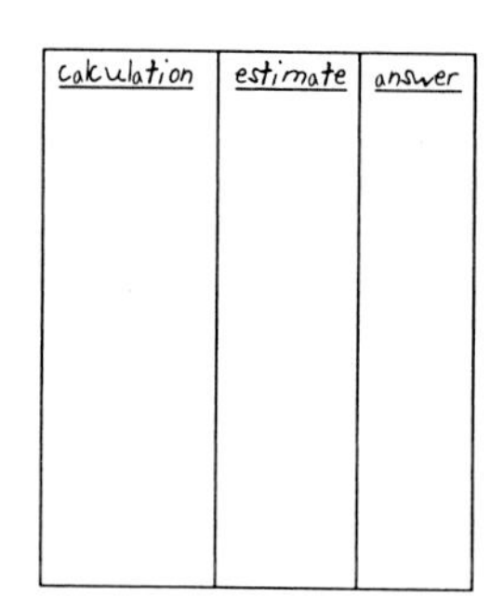

On your calculator, key in the calculation [1] [÷] [2] [=].

Write the calculation and your answer on your record sheet.

Mettan pressed
[1] [÷] [2] [=]
and got 0·5 .

calculation	estimate	answer
1÷2		0·5

You are now going to divide that answer by 2. Before you do so, try to guess what the answer will be, and write it in the estimate column.

Try it on the calculator and write the answer in the answer column.

Mettan thought it would be 0·1, but it was 0·25.

calculation	estimate	answer
1 ÷ 2		0·5
0·5 ÷ 2	0·1	0·25

Each time you get an answer you should:

- record it on your sheet
- write the new calculation in the 'calculation' column
- estimate what you will get if you divide that answer by 2 again
- divide it by 2

When you have gone as far as the calculator can go, try again, with 2 ÷ 4, 4 ÷ 8 and 8 ÷ 16.

What do you notice?

Can you explain what is happening?

Questions

Do your answers get bigger or smaller?

Do different types of calculator produce identical answers?

Why is that?

What happens with these divisions?

$1 \div 4$ $4 \div 16$ $16 \div 64$

$1 \div 3$ $3 \div 9$ $9 \div 27$

If on your calculator these divisions all end with zero, why is that?

Do the divisions **really** end with 0?

Suggestions

Try this activity with the help of a spreadsheet.

On your calculator press

Keep dividing by 2 and record your results.

Now take a piece of paper and cut it into two pieces. On the calculator divide 1 by the number of pieces of paper you have. What do you notice?

Now cut each of these pieces of paper in two. Divide 1 by the number of pieces of paper you have. What do you notice?

Carry on like this. Do you ever end up with no paper?

Fingers and Thumbs

for 1 or more people

You need sticky paper

Write numbers on scraps of sticky paper and stick them on your thumbs and fingers — as in the picture. (Make sure you get the numbers on the correct fingers.)

1 Add the numbers on both thumbs, both little fingers, and so on.

What do you notice?

2 Add all of the numbers on your left hand and all the numbers on your right hand.

What is the total on each?

What is the difference between these totals?

3 What is the total of the numbers on all of the little fingers in the class added together?

4 What is the total of the numbers on the left thumbs of all the people at your table?

5 Make up more investigations using different fingers and different numbers of people.

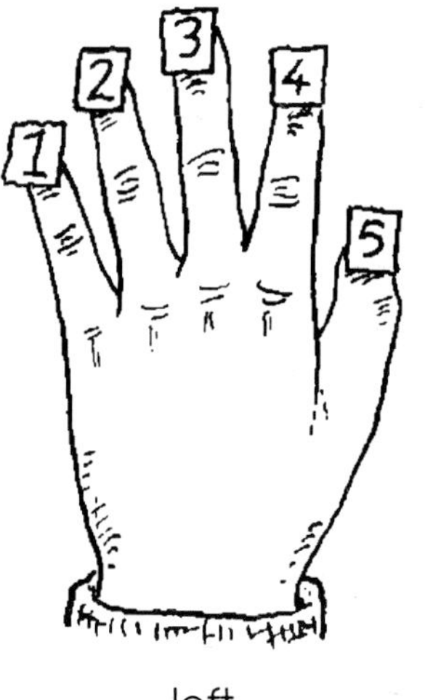

left

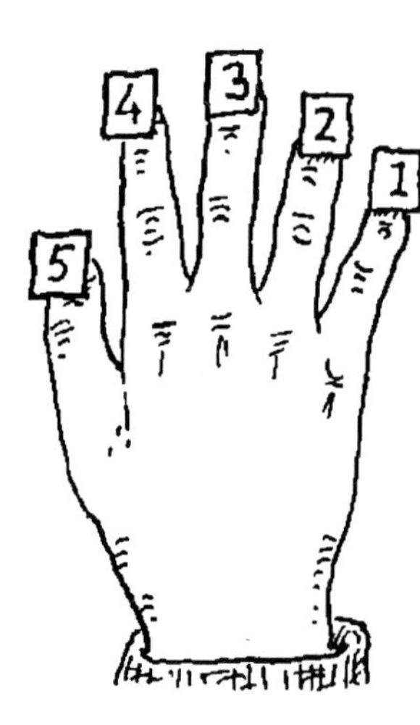

right

Questions

If *everyone* in the school were to join in, what would the total for middle fingers be?

What about the total for right-hand middle fingers?

What if *everyone* in your family/town/country joined in?

What would the totals be?

Variations

Use a different set of numbers on each finger.

Use amounts of money on each finger — for example, 1p, 2p, 5p . . .

Try to invent some activities using these numbers and multiplication, division or subtraction.

Roll-a-Number

for 2 people

You need calculator
1–6 dice

Set the calculator to 10 and agree a target number under 100.

Player 1:

- ➤ roll the dice and say the number you get
- ➤ do an operation on the number in the calculator display (which is 10 at the moment); you can use:
  - — the dice-number
  - — and any of these keys:

Player 2:

- ➤ you do the same thing

Both players:

- ➤ carry on taking turns like this until one of you lands on the target number

Sally and Mettan set the calculator to 10 and chose a target of 69.

Sally rolled the dice and got 6.

She pressed [+] [6][0] [=] and got 70.

The calculator now showed 70.

Mettan rolled the dice and got 5.

He pressed [−] [0][·][5] [=] and got 69·5.

Questions

What operation would you do if:
— your target was 100
— the calculator showed 25
— and your dice-throw gave you a 4?

Can you make up some similar questions for your friends?

Variations

Use target numbers as high as 1000.

Start with 999 in your calculator and aim for a target below 100.

You could ban the use of one of the operation keys.

For example, you might decide you could only use the [×], [÷] and [−] keys.

Dartboard Scores

for 1 or more people

You need paper and pencil

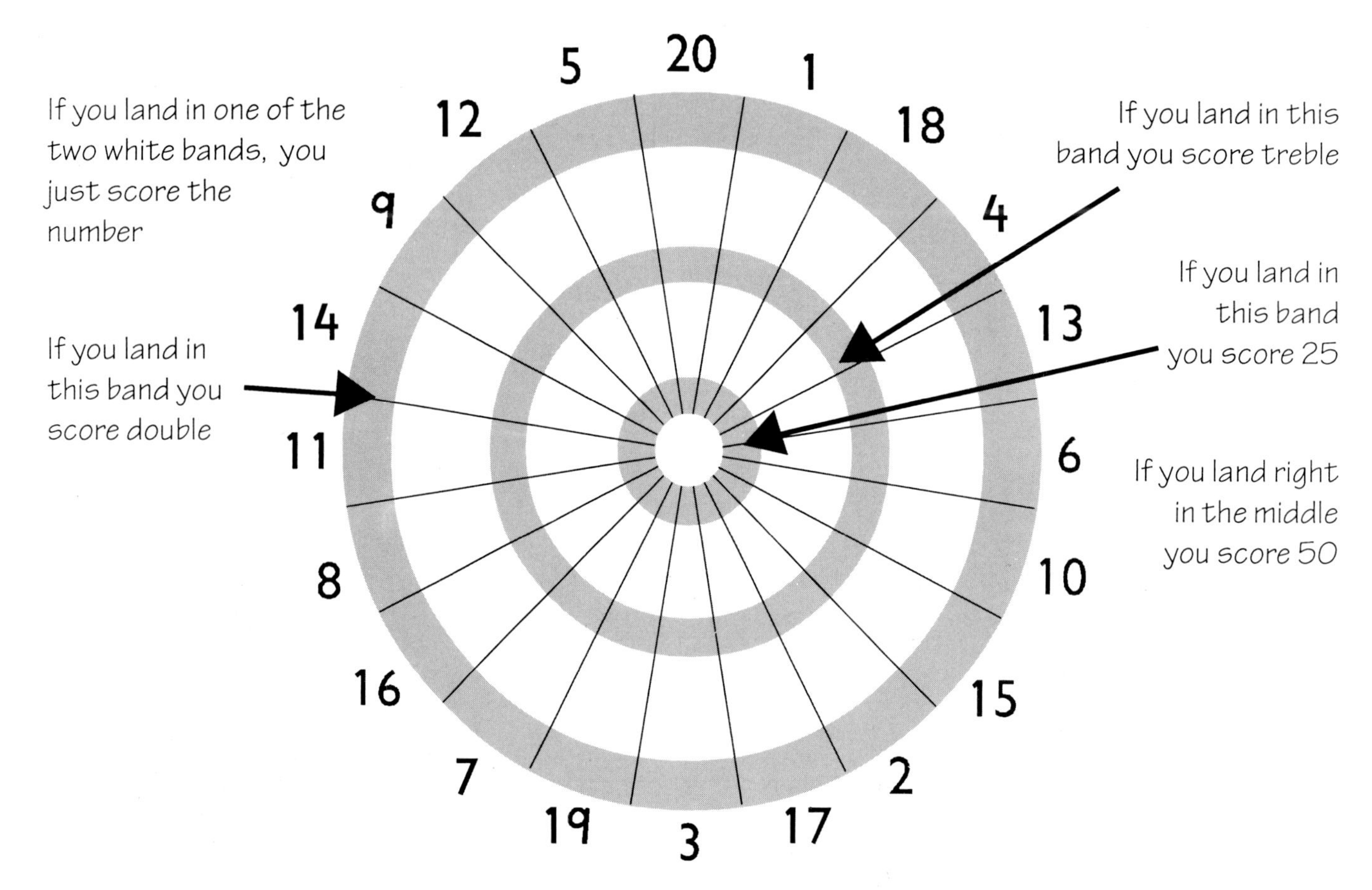

Imagine a player throws just one dart.

1 What is the lowest score possible?

2 And what is the highest score possible?

3 Is it possible to score all numbers between the lowest and highest score?

4 Which scores can be made in more than one way?

Questions

What numbers over 20 can't you make with one dart?

Why is that?

Which scores between 1 and 20 can you **only** make with a single dart?

Do these have anything in common?

Pick any number. What are all the ways of making that number with one dart?

With two darts? Three darts?

Suggestions

Try the same investigations using two darts or three darts.

Draw a real dartboard, using compasses, a ruler, and a protractor. Be as accurate as possible.

Dartboard 301

for 2 or 3 people

You need 2 dice
pencil and paper

Your aim is to be the first person to reach exactly 301.

Take turns to:

- roll both dice
- use the two dice-numbers, with any operation (+, ×, − or ÷) to produce a score
- roll **one** of the dice again

  If you get a 1 or 2 then your score stays the same

  If you get 3 or 4 then you double your score

  If you get 5 or 6 then you treble your score
- record your total score

Keep taking turns like this and adding your new score to your old one.

The game is over when someone reaches 301 exactly or everybody has gone bust.

RULES

Your score before doubling or trebling must be 20 or lower (20 is the highest number on a dartboard).

Your score must be a whole number.

If you go over 301 then you have gone bust and you lose.

Sally threw a 5 and a 4.

She could score

$5 \times 4 = 20$ or $5 + 4 = 9$

or $5 - 4 = 1$

($5 \div 4$ is not allowed as it doesn't produce a whole number.)

Questions

Can you work out an easy way to treble 12 in your head?

Or treble 19?

Can you add the scores in your head without writing a calculation?

If someone has 165 and scores 39, what is their new score?

Can you explain how you do additions in your head?

Variations

Allow single scores greater than 20, such as 6×6.

Use a lower or higher target than 301.

Start at 301 and aim to end on exactly zero.

Play in teams so you can help each other.

Landing Zone

for 2 or 3 people

You need a dice
a copy of the Landing Zone grid
paper and pencil for keeping scores

Your aim is to be the first person to reach as close as possible to100.

In turn, players should:

➤ roll the dice so that it lands on the grid

➤ look at the number on the dice and the number that the dice has landed on

➤ use these two numbers, with any operation (+, ×, – or ÷) to produce a score

Mettan threw a 5 which landed on 3.

He could score

$5 \times 3 = 15$ or $5 + 3 = 8$ or

$5 - 3 = 2$ or $5 \div 3 = 1{\cdot}\dot{6}$

➤ record your score

All players:

➤ keep taking turns, and adding your new score to your old one — you must aim to reach as close to 100 as you can

The game is over when someone has reached 100 or everybody has gone bust.

RULES

If you miss the grid when you roll the dice you score zero.

If the dice lands touching more than one number you can choose any of those numbers.

If you go over 100 then you have gone bust and you lose.

7	5	2	3	2
2	8	1	9	10
6	7	12	0	7
2	1	4	2	5
3	6	3	8	3
4	14	6	11	9

Roll-a-Square

for 2 people

You need 3 dice
a copy of the Roll-a-Square grid
2 sets of counters

Take turns to:

- roll all three dice
- use the three numbers, with any operations (+, ×, – or ÷) to produce **one** of the numbers on the grid
- cover that number on the grid with a counter in your colour

The winner could be:

— the person who covers the most squares on the grid

— the first person to cover four in a line

— or the person who . . .

Make up your own rule to decide who wins.

Sally threw 5, 3 and 4 . She could make

$(5 \times 4) + 3 = 23$ or $5 + 4 + 3 = 12$

or $(5 - 4) + 3 = 4$ or $(5 \times 4) - 3 = 17$

or lots of other numbers. She chose 12.

Variation

Design a
different-sized grid, or
a different-shaped grid.

1	2	3	4	5	6
7	8	9	10	11	12
13	14	15	16	17	18
19	20	21	22	23	24
25	26	27	28	29	30
31	32	33	34	35	36

How Many?

for 1 or more people

How many of the following can you count in your classroom or home?

children	chairs	prisms	cm
adults	chair legs	cubes	cm^2
hands	tables	cuboids	m
thumbs	table legs	words	m^2
toes	years	letters	m^3
fingers	months	ideas	km
teeth	weeks	dreams	g
bones	days	sandwiches	kg
nails	hours	sweets	ml
brothers	minutes	numbers	litres
sisters	seconds	names	°C
friends	squares	sounds	°F
parents	circles	pound coins	mph
animals	triangles	pence	kph

Variation

Make a list of things that there is only one of in your home/classroom.

Questions

What about in your school or your town or in the whole world?

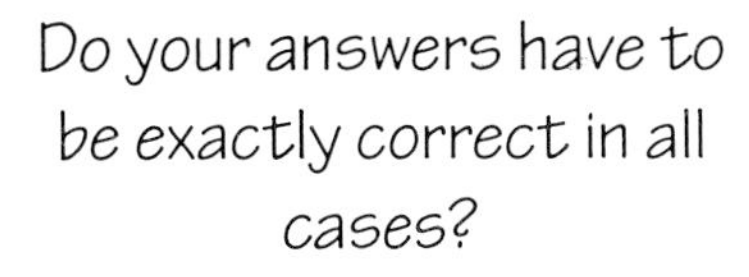

Could you estimate answers for another room, or house, without having to go and ask for details?

Does multiplication always provide a faster way of counting?

Why?

Words to Help You

Consecutive

This means 'next-door'.

2, 3 and 4 are consecutive numbers;
3, 6 and 9 are consecutive multiples of 3;
5, 7, 9 and 11 are consecutive odd numbers.

Digit

The digits are 0, 1, 2, 3, 4, 5, 6, 7, 8 and 9.

5 is a single-digit number;
23 is a two-digit number;
635 is a three-digit number.

Multiple

Multiples are the numbers in the multiplication tables.

Some multiples of 2 are 4, 6, 12 and 20;
15 and 10 are both multiples of 5.

Negative number

These are the numbers you reach if you go below 0.

6 5 4 3 2 1 0 −1 −2 −3 −4 −5 −6

Operation

When you do something to a number you operate on it. The four main operations are addition, subtraction, multiplication and division.

Spreadsheet

A spreadsheet is a computer program that helps you organise facts and figures, and does operations for you.

Excel is one spreadsheet you may use in school.

The Mathematics Covered in the Activities

This chart gives you some idea of what mathematics you will be learning and practising when you do these activities and their variations

	Brick Walls	Subtraction Walls	Bingo	Make 10	Make 10 Challenge	Quick as a Flash	Tables Chase	Odds and Evens Race	Some Sum	Magic Squares	Doubling	Double Digit	Sharing	Fingers and Thumbs	Roll-a-Number	Dartboard Scores	Dartboard 301	Landing Zone	Roll-a-Square	How Many?
properties of number	☆	☆						☆					☆							
place value			☆									☆	☆		☆					
estimating and rounding													☆	☆	☆					☆
fractions and decimals	☆		☆		☆	☆	☆		☆		☆		☆		☆					
addition and subtraction to 20	☆	☆		☆	☆	☆			☆	☆	☆	☆		☆	☆	☆	☆	☆	☆	
addition and subtraction to 100	☆	☆	☆	☆	☆	☆	☆	☆	☆	☆	☆	☆		☆	☆	☆	☆	☆	☆	☆
addition and subtraction over 100	☆	☆	☆				☆		☆		☆	☆		☆	☆	☆	☆			☆
multiplication and division to 100 and over						☆	☆	☆	☆		☆	☆	☆	☆	☆	☆	☆	☆	☆	☆
doubling and halving											☆		☆	☆		☆	☆			☆
reasoning about numbers	☆	☆	☆					☆	☆	☆	☆	☆	☆	☆	☆	☆				☆
patterns and relationships	☆	☆		☆	☆				☆	☆	☆	☆				☆				☆
generalising about numbers	☆	☆						☆		☆		☆	☆							☆
making predictions	☆	☆								☆		☆	☆	☆						☆
working systematically	☆	☆		☆	☆					☆	☆	☆	☆	☆		☆	☆		☆	☆
working collaboratively			☆	☆	☆	☆	☆	☆	☆		☆	☆			☆		☆	☆	☆	

8 5 7

Acknowledgements

We would like to thank the following for helping trial these games and activities:

David Armstrong and Long Buckby Junior School, Northamptonshire

Toni Ashman and Hazelwood Junior School, London

Frances Bestley and the South London Science and Technology Centre

Keith Cadman and the Jennie Lee Community and Professional Centre

Barbara Carr and Cranford House School, Oxon

Muriel Chester and the Southwark BEAM Group

Peter Clarke, Advisory Teacher for Mathematics

Diana Cobden and the Dorset Mathematics Advisory Team

Marion Cranmer and Dog Kennel Hill Primary School, London

Tejinder Dhingra and Culloden Primary School and Hearing Impaired Unit

Marie Donagher and St Joseph's Primary School, London

Rosemary Hafeez and the Croydon BEAM Group

JE Harris and Henham and Ugley CP School, Bishops Stortford

Jenny Jeffcoat, Mike Wadsley and Smitham Primary School, Surrey

Val Jerram and the Brighton and Hove BEAM Group

Kathy Lawrence and Little Common CP School, Bexhill-on-Sea

Ellika McAuley and Swiss Cottage School, London

Isabel McNaught-Davis and the East Sussex BEAM Group

Adèle Markey and Bury and Whitefield Jewish Primary School, Lancashire

Sadie Maxwell and Brentnall CP School, Salford

Olive Millington and Reed First School, Hertfordshire

Ceri Morgan, Justin Schiffman and Hagley First School, West Midlands

Janet Parfitt and Balfour Junior School, Brighton

Jane Prothero and Grimes Dyke Primary School, Leeds

Susan Saunders, Debra Turner, Andy Wilson, Eileen Campbell, Helen Emerson and Bevendean Primary School, Brighton

Ken Scott and St Martin's CE Primary School, Wolverhampton

Wendy Spratling and St Alban's CE Primary School, Wolverhampton

Aimee Warren and Bishop Winnington Ingram CE Primary School, Ruislip

Carolyn Weston, Jane Hadfield and St Peter and St Paul Primary School, Bexhill-on-Sea

Other BEAM Books You May Enjoy

Calculators in Their Hands

by Fran Mosley

Ever heard someone say calculators make you lazy?

Well, it's not true. The calculator games and explorations in this book really stretch your mathematical powers — whether you are aged 6 or 60, 9 or 90. For instance, can you get from 0 to 22 in steps of 3? Or from 5 to 100 in just three stages? How do you make the display show 1512 without pressing any odd numbers? Or find the cube root of 343?

Some of the games and activities are quite easy, and others are harder. But they are all fun. And you'll learn lots of mathematics in the process.

Calculators in Their Hands contains 23 games and activities for children, alone and with a companion, using calculators and everyday equipment such as pencils and paper.

Cards on the Table

by Fran Mosley

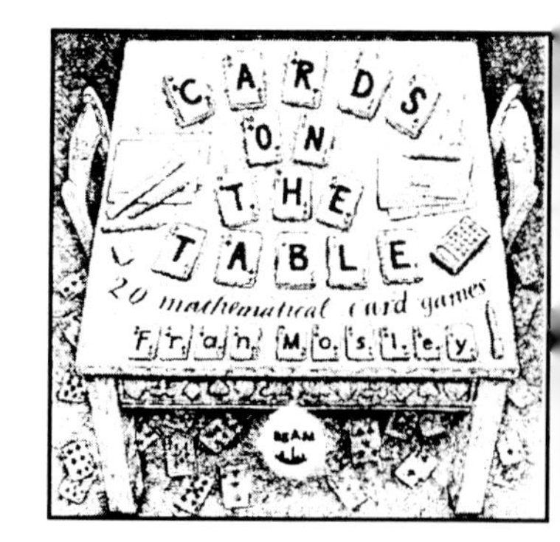

100 calculations in a minute!

Did you think that only computers could think that fast? You can do it too! (Well, nearly.) Playing these card games gets you doing all sorts of things with numbers — adding and subtracting them, working out factors, aiming for some numbers and avoiding others. The more you play them, the faster you become, and the more you develop your intuitive and flexible thinking skills — the mark of a real mathematician.

Cards on the Table contains 20 games for children to play with ordinary playing cards.

Next in the series:

Casting the Dice

A collection of exciting games to play with dice.